Contents

CW01651354

LEARNING

Transcripts for the Hennings Haus programmes are available at www.4learning.co.uk

We are always pleased to receive constructive comments and suggestions about both the series and the support materials. Please write to me at the address below.

Anne Fleck Education Officer 4Learning PO Box 100 Warwick CV34 6TZ

Hennings Haus is a series of five programmes for young learners of German. It is set in Germany and introduces Henning and groups of children in settings that are sometimes firmly rooted in real life and at other times stretch the imagination of the audience.

- The programmes and the accompanying teachers' guide aim to introduce a wide range of language structures and vocabulary, which give viewers practice in the skills needed at the early stages of language learning:
  - listening for fun and information
  - speaking in a context
  - a guided introduction to reading and writing
  - information about countries where German is spoken.

- The guide is divided into two sections:
  - teachers' notes that provide key vocabulary and suggestions for activities
  - pupil activity sheets to consolidate language and extend pupils' knowledge of Germany and German life.

- The transcripts of the programmes will be published on the 4Learning website.

Language content

Programme 1
Wie heißt du?

Introductions and greetings; the alphabet; numbers 1–20; ten colours
Recognition of pronouns ich/du/er/wir; verb pattern ich .... e (eg ich wohne); exception: ich bin

Programme 2
Auf die Plätze, fertig, los!

Recognise times; describe/ask about hobbies/sports; play a board game
Verbs used with hobbies and sports; verb pattern du .... st (eg du wohnst) exception: du bist

Programme 3
Der falsche Rucksack!

Recognise and use weather phrases; travel and transport; clothes; picnic food
Verb sein; ich/du ... e/st with more verbs; plurals of nouns

Programme 4
So ein Lärm!

Pets and other animals; the noises animals make
Plural of present tense verbs; third person singular present tense verbs

Programme 5
Hennings Geburtstag

Days; recognise and say birthdays; family members; handle money; organise a party; numbers above 20
Present tense of haben

Each programme contains a rap sung by the children and Henning. Your pupils will be able to learn the rap – and to write others.

Preparatory Work

Before you watch any of the programmes, ask pupils to make small cards with the colours to be seen and heard in Programme 1 and with the numbers 1–20 on them. The children should cut their cards up and practise their numbers and colours intensively for a few minutes with you and in groups for several weeks before they start to watch the programmes.

Throughout the pupils' worksheets, you will find references to websites and Internet challenges. You may want to check sites out before letting children work on them. You will find an extensive library of information about Germany and German life as well as life in other German-speaking countries at these web addresses:

http://www.odci.gov/cia/publications/factbook/geos/gm.html

http://www.tricounty.esu6.org/german/w_extra.htm

http://sps.k12.mo.us/khs/german/gerlinks.htm

http://www.transparent.com/languagepages/ger/overview.htm

http://www.transparent.com/wotd/today/german_wotd.htm

http://www.deutsche-kultur-international.de/i/eideuaus.htm

http://www.bremen.de/info/bremen/Willkommene.html

http://www.fcb.de/de/home/0,3833,,00.html

Good information is, of course, also available from printed texts: most bookshops now carry a stock of foreign language books for children. If you live near a Goethe-Institut, you will find its library invaluable.

Wie heißt du?

The story

A group of children meet Henning, who has fallen off his bike and forgotten his name. When we have learned the children's names they are set the challenge of finding Henning's house. A search of the neighbourhood reveals it to be a converted railway goods truck.

Learning outcomes

This programme introduces pupils to:

- introductions and greetings
- the alphabet
- numbers
- ten colours

In the pupils' worksheets, some illustrations are designed so that they can be photocopied to a larger format where the teacher feels this is appropriate.

Contents

Pupils will also learn to recognise the pronouns ich/du/er /wir and the verb pattern ich followed by the ending -e (as in ich wohne) and ich bin.

Key vocabulary

- Greetings:
  Guten Tag! ▪ Hallo! ▪ Wie geht's? ▪ Danke, gut.
  Danke, besser. ▪ Tschüs! ▪ Auf Wiedersehen!
  Ja ▪ Nein ▪ Entschuldigung ▪ Tut mir leid
- Question forms:
  Wer bist du? ▪ Ich bin… ▪ Wer ist …? ▪ Das ist ….
  Wie heißt du? ▪ Ich heiße …
  Wo wohnst du? ▪ Ich wohne …
- Directions:
  rechts ▪ links ▪ geradeaus
- Exclamations:
  Schau! ▪ Schaut! ▪ Kommt! ▪ Sehr gut ▪ Das ist richtig

Before viewing

- ☐ Pin sheets of paper – some long-wise and some cross-wise – on a display area that all the children can see. Some sheets should have a large rectangle on them – this is Henning's house. Some should have an outline of a man's shape on them – this is Henning.

- ☐ Give the children in groups of four a challenge: to draw what they think a really weird person and his really weird house would look like. They can make their drawings from collage paper or from newsprint or from wool or other craft materials; they can each draw one part of the house and of Henning and then stick all the bits together to make one identikit picture.

- ☐ Ask the children to imagine they were meeting Henning for the first time: what would they say to each other? What would Henning want to know about them? (Suggestions: they might ask people's names and ages, where they come from, what they are doing here, etc.) Get the children to make speech bubbles of their suggestions and pin them up on the display board. As they watch the programmes, they should tick off topics they suggested as they appear.

- ☐ If you haven't already done so, teach children the very first things you have to be able to say if you want to get to know someone, so that they will recognise language at the start of the first programme.

- ☐ This may lead on to a discussion of names in German, and you might want to pause a moment to let the children know the top ten boys' and girls' names in Germany in 1997 (the latest available statistics):

Language and culture

Die beliebtesten Vornamen

Jungen	**Mädchen**
1. Alexander	1. Maria/Marie
2. Maximilian	2. Sophia/Sophie
3. Lukas	3. Julia
4. Philipp	4. Laura
5. Daniel	5. Anna/Anne
6. Jan	6. Sara(h)
7. Florian	7. Lisa
8. Niklas	8. Katharina
9. Felix	9. Vanessa
10. Dominik	10. Michelle

During viewing

- ☐ Watch the first part of the programme, which introduces Henning. Pause the video and let the children decide whether any of their drawings of Henning are close to what they see on the screen.

- ☐ Replay the alphabet as many times as necessary and then play games with the children:
  - spell the names of people in the class in German and encourage them to guess when they hear their own name
  - photocopy the list of names on page 4, spell names from it and ask the children to guess which names you are spelling
  - spell the names of famous people (film stars, singers, footballers, etc) and again ask the children to guess who they are.

- ☐ Finally, help the children to spell their own given name and surname in German. Do Worksheet 1.

- ☐ Watch the second part of the video and practise with children saying which town and country they live in. Then put up pictures of different types of houses. Ask the children to practise saying what kind of house they live in.

- ☐ Watch the next part of the video in which children say numbers and colours. Encourage children to learn to describe their own house: Das ist unser Bungalow – Nummer neun. Die Tür ist rot. Play number games such as bingo and snap; do simple additions and other sums using number cards. Do Worksheet 2.

- ☐ Watch the next part of the video in which the children look for Hennings Haus. Make a note of the description given of the house. Go over colours and do Worksheet 3.

- ☐ Then watch the last part of the video and decide which of the children's drawings is closest to the 'real' Henning's house. Do Worksheets 4 and 5.

After viewing

- ☐ Once the children have seen the programme in sections and have completed the worksheets that accompany each section, show the whole programme. They should be able to take part in certain sections of the programme:
  - reciting the alphabet along with the children in the programme
  - saying the kind of 'house' each person lives in as they say it
  - saying numbers as they appear on the screen
  - saying directions as they hear them
  - saying colours as they appear on the screen
  - repeating the rap along with Henning and the children.

- ☐ Follow-up to Worksheet 1: on the website [http://www.userpage.chemie.fu-berlin.de/diverse/doc/kfz.html] you will find car number plates showing the abbreviations for all German cities and regions.

Arbeitsbogen 1

Name ....

Datum ....

Aufgabe 1

Zeichne und illustriere dein eigenes Alphabet!

Design and illustrate your own alphabet!

a b c d e f g h i j k l m

n o p q r s t u v w x y z

Now play alphabet games with the teacher and in your group.

Aufgabe 2

Hier ist ein Alphabetquiz: Aus welchen Ländern kommen diese Autos?

Here's a quiz about the alphabet: what countries do these cars come from?

CH D Ö

Was für Autos sind das? Wie sagt man auf Deutsch?

What makes of car are these?

How do you say them in German?

VW BMW MB

Aus welchen Städten kommen diese Autos?

Which German cities do these cars come from?

D HH 4872 D M 9219 D F 9898

Challenge: look around your school and the area where you live: can you see any cars with German numbers? Where do they come from?

Arbeitsbogen 2

Name ....

Datum ....

Aufgabe 1

Wieviele? Im Klassenzimmer zähl:

How many are there? In the classroom, count:

die Fenster

die Türe

die Mädchen

die Jungen

die Computer

Aufgabe 2

Schau auf die Landkarte Deutschlands. Wieviele gibt es?

Look at the map of Germany on page 41. How many are there of these?

- Länder
- Flüsse
- Städte, die mit B anfangen
- Städte, die mit H anfangen

Aufgabe 3

Buchstaben-Quadrat

Wordsearch – find the 16 Länder (states) in the grid:

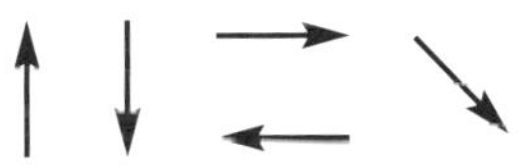

B	A	D	E	N	S	C	H	H	W	I	G
W	Ü	R	T	T	E	M	B	E	R	G	R
S	V	K	H	S	A	Q	S	S	V	H	U
S	B	O	H	M	P	G	W	S	L	B	B
S	N	T	R	U	X	R	Y	E	O	O	N
A	G	S	F	P	J	U	I	N	R	R	E
A	E	A	B	D	O	B	K	J	S	Z	L
R	G	C	B	N	E	M	E	R	B	T	K
L	B	H	G	I	X	A	M	O	E	L	C
A	H	S	O	O	V	H	Z	E	Y	A	E
N	R	E	Y	A	B	H	R	E	R	H	M
D	I	N	U	E	B	E	R	L	I	N	I
N	I	E	H	R	D	R	O	N	W	A	Z
N	I	E	D	E	R	A	W	R	R	N-	N
Z	L	A	F	P	S	A	C	H	S	E	N
N	E	G	I	W	S	E	L	H	C	S	O
G	C	Ü	N	E	G	N	I	R	Ü	H	T
-D	N	A	L	N	I	E	H	R	E	C	Ü
H	W	E	S	T	F	A	L	E	N	A	N
H	O	L	S	T	E	I	N	E	N	S	W
B	R	A	N	D	E	N	B	U	R	G	Ü

Internet Challenge: find out how these German football teams got on last week. Make a wall display with the team colours and mark the scores every week: Mönchengladbach, FC Bayern

eins
zwei
drei
vier
fünf
sechs
sieben
acht
neun
zehn
elf
zwölf
dreizehn
vierzehn
fünfzehn
sechzehn
siebzehn
achtzehn
neunzehn
zwanzig

Arbeitsbogen 3

Name ....

Datum ....

Aufgabe 1

Welche Farbe haben diese Fahnen? Verwende den Code!

What colours are these flags? Use the code!

1 rot
2 blau
3 weiß
4 gold
5 schwarz

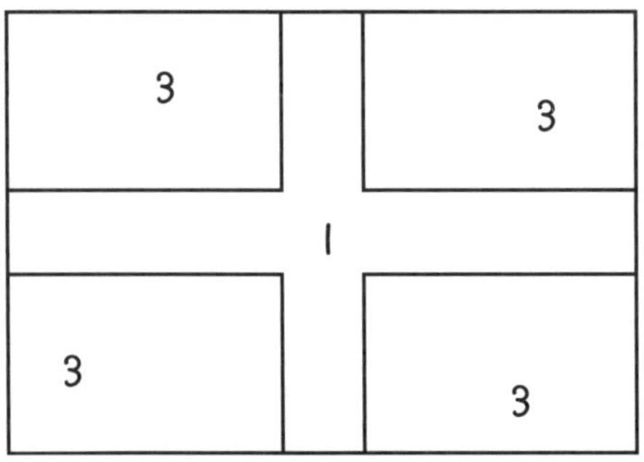

England

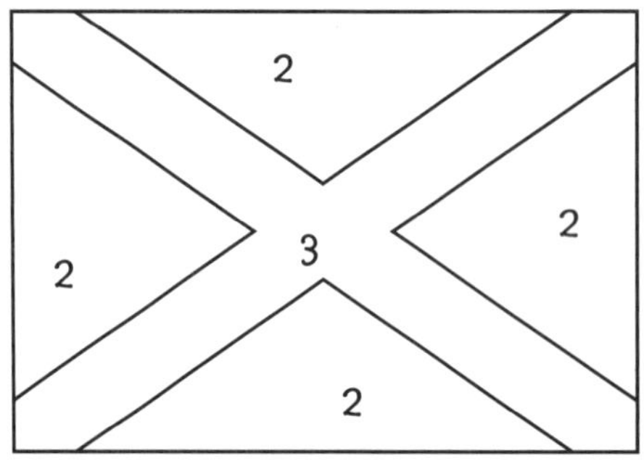

Schottland

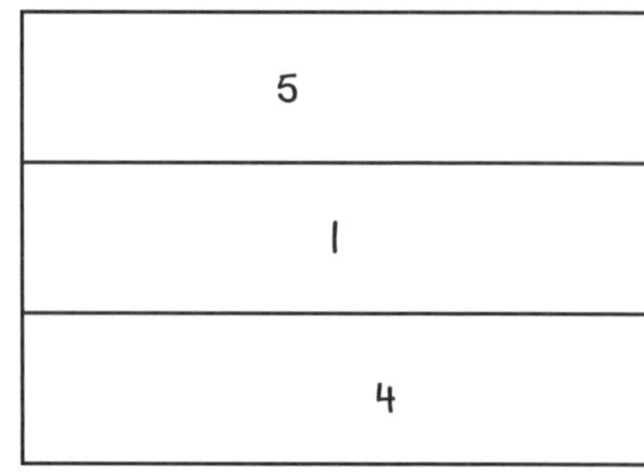

Deutschland

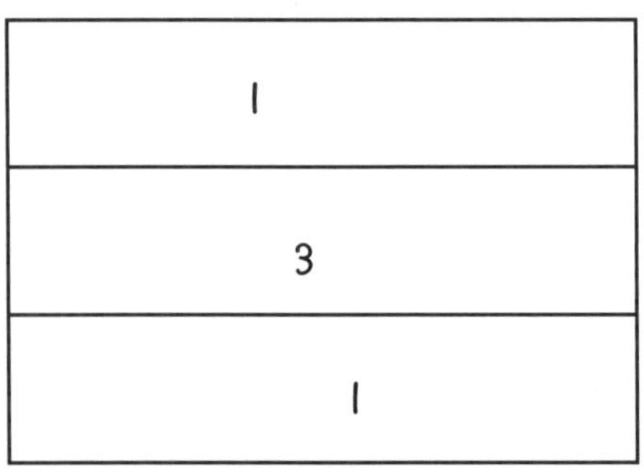

Österreich

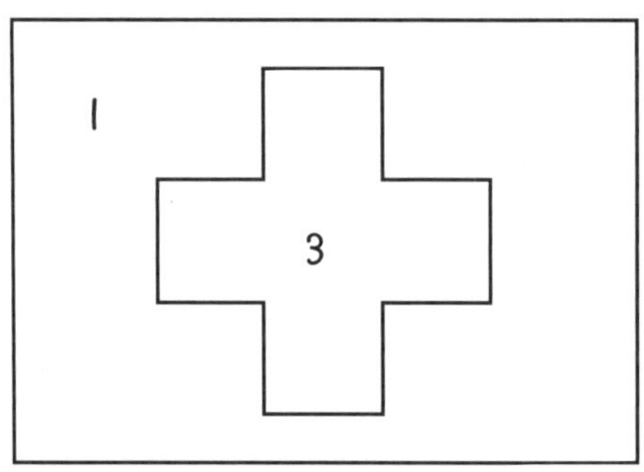

die Schweiz

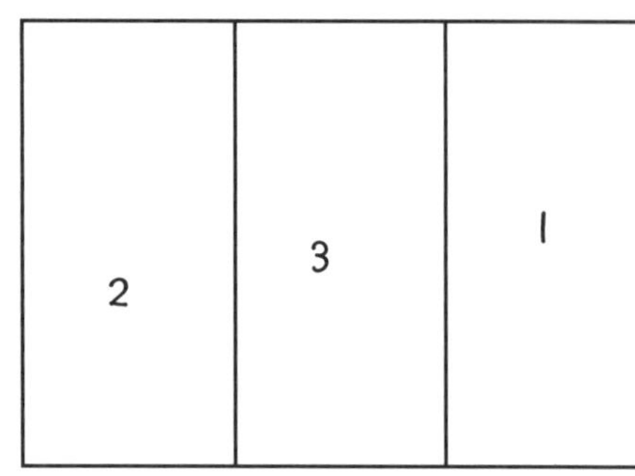

Frankreich

Aufgabe 2

Welche Farbe haben diese Früchte und Gemüse?

Which colour are these fruit and vegetables?

Die Bananen sind ....

Die Orangen sind ....

Die Erdbeeren sind ....

Die Bohnen sind ....

Die Weintrauben sind ....

gelb	blau
schwarz	orange
grün	weiß
rot	grau

Internet challenge: what colours are the coats of arms – die Wappen – of the 16 German states? Check out: http://sps.k12.mo.us/khs/german/gerlinks.htm

If you have time, find out about other German coats of arms.

Quiz: Can you do something if it's verboten? Would you be pleased if you were called a Wunderkind? What would you do with a Glockenspiel?

Arbeitsbogen 4

Name ....

Datum ....

Aufgabe 1
Wer bin ich?
Who am I?

Ich bin ein Physiker – ich heiße ....

Ich bin eine Tennisspielerin – ich heiße ....

Ich bin ein Komponist – ich heiße ....

Ich bin ein Schauspieler – ich heiße ....

Ich bin ein Fußballspieler – ich heiße ....

Aufgabe 2
Find deinen Partner oder deine Partnerin!
Find your partner! He or she must have the same name and age as on your card.

Brigitte 11	Martin 10	Monika 12	Franz 9
Brigitte 11	Martin 10	Monika 12	Franz 9

Wie heißt du? Ich heiße .... Wie alt bist du? Ich bin ....

Aufgabe 3
Schau im Wörterbuch nach. Welcher deutsche Titel passt am besten zu welchem englischen Titel?
Look in the dictionary. Which German title matches each English title?

Aschenputtel	Little Red Riding Hood
der Froschkönig	The Pied Piper
Schneewittchen	The Frog Prince
Dornröschen	Cinderella
der Rattenfänger von Hameln	Snow White
Rotkäppchen	Sleeping Beauty

Challenge: which one of Santa's reindeer has a name that means 'thunder' in German and which has a name that means 'lightning'?

Arbeitsbogen 5

Name ....

Datum ....

Aufgabe 1
Lies den Brief von einem deutschen Jungen. Er will einen ,,Keypal" finden. Was kannst du über ihn herausfinden?
Read this letter from a German boy who wants a 'keypal' – an Internet penpal. What can you find out about him?

Ich heiße Klaus. Ich bin zwölf. Ich wohne in Leipzig in Deutschland. Und du? Wie alt bist du? Wo wohnst du?

Ich habe einen Bruder aber keine Schwester. Und du?
Ich spiele gern mit dem Computer und gehe gern ins Kino. Was sind deine Hobbys?

Klaus
:-)

Aufgabe 2
Beantworte die Fragen, die Klaus dir gestellt hat. Dann füll das Anmeldeformular aus, um einen ,,Keypal" zu finden.
Answer Klaus's questions about you. Then fill in this keypal application form:

Name	....
Vorname(n)	....
Alter	....
Wohnort	....
Hobbys	....

Aufgabe 3
Was bedeuten diese Wörter auf Englisch?
What do these German words mean?

braun	kommen	trinken ....
Mutter	lernen	Milch ....
Sohn	Familie	Wasser ....

Jetzt bist du dran! Wieviele deutsche Wörter kannst du finden, die englischen Wörtern gleichen?
Now it's your turn! How many German words can you find that sound or look like English words and mean the same?

Challenge: Have a look at the shelves in your local supermarkets and make a note of any foods you see that come from German-speaking countries – Germany, Switzerland or Austria. If you can get empty food packets or draw the foods, you can make a wall display of typical German foods.

Auf die Plätze, fertig, los!

The story

The children gather at Henning's House after school and he challenges them to beat him in a race against the clock. He then uses his magic to help his friends win all their races at the school's sports day.

Learning outcomes

This programme introduces pupils to:

- clock times
- words for hobbies and sports and saying how you feel about them
- playing a board game

Pupils will also learn to recognise and use verbs to describe hobbies and sports, recognise the verb pattern 'du' followed by the ending -st (as in du wohnst) and du bist.

acht Uhr

halb sechs

Key vocabulary

- Time:
  Wieviel Uhr ist es? ▪ Wie spät ist es? ▪ Es ist ein Uhr
  Es ist zwei Uhr (etc) ▪ Es ist halb sechs
- Sports/hobbies:
  Was machst du gern? ▪ Was ist dein Hobby? ▪ Was sind deine Hobbys? ▪ Fußball spielen ▪ Rad fahren
  tanzen ▪ schwimmen ▪ laufen ▪ Skateboard fahren
  Inline Skates fahren ▪ Musik hören ▪ lesen
  fotografieren ▪ fernsehen ▪ ich fahre gern Rad
  ich tanze gern ▪ ich schwimme gern
  ich spiele gern Fußball ▪ ich laufe gern
  ich fahre gern mit dem Skateboard
  ich fahre gern mit den Inline Skates
  Fußball ist blöd ▪ prima ▪ langweilig ▪ toll
- Board game:
  ich habe gewonnen ▪ du hast verloren
  du schummelst ▪ das Rennen ▪ Start ▪ Ziel
- Exclamations:
  das ist falsch ▪ das stimmt ▪ schnell
  schneller ▪ langsam

Before viewing

- Using a large clock face, teach the children first the time on the hour, then the question forms Wieviel Uhr ist es? and Wie spät ist es? and then halb + a number. To practise times, from a newspaper read them the names of TV programmes that start on the hour – eg Brookside – and let them fill in the time – acht Uhr. Then do the same for programmes that start on the half hour: Hollyoaks – halb sechs.

- Ask the children to make flashcards for you showing a range of sports and hobbies. Work on these six at a time, getting the children first of all to repeat after you the German names and then playing a variety of flashcard games: say the names on the cards and put them face down on the table. See if pupils can remember which card was which; hide the cards behind your back, jumble them up and them hold them up blank side towards the pupils and ask them to guess which one you are looking at; hold the cards up one at a time and say a name – if you say the right name, pupils say 'richtig', but if you say a wrong name they say 'falsch'.

- Ask each of the pupils to pick out three or four sports or hobbies they like and teach them to say their opinion of these, using the 'gern' expression first and later the adjectives. Pupils should, after oral practice of these expressions, draw their own hobbies and sports and put captions on their drawings showing what they think of them.

Language and culture

- When pupils first write in German, it has to be pointed out to them that in some ways German can be very easy to say because some words sound very like English: Schuh, Arm, Vater, Wind, blau, Hand, Garten, Bruder, lernen, Bus, bringen, etc. This is because English belongs to the same family of languages as German.

- However, writing is different and there are some things you have to watch out for: there's the Umlaut for one thing, which changes the sound, yet the word looks the same – Ärme, grün, Fräulein, etc. Then there's the ei/ie rule – klein/Brief. And they also have to remember that nouns have a capital letter: Milch, Hand, Morgen, etc.

During viewing

- Ask the children to watch the first part of the programme, in which they should be able to understand the times as they hear them. They can then do Worksheets 1 and 2. Once pupils have watched the next two sections of the programme, in the school playground and at Henning's house, they can complete Worksheet 3. Pupils can do Worksheet 4 after Henning's challenge. Worksheet 5 can be completed at any time and can be given for homework. If children have access to the Internet at home, they might want to visit the Bayern München website:
  http://www.fcb.de/de/home/0,3833,,00.html

After viewing

- Children will need some time to complete the worksheet activities. They should then have the opportunity to watch the programme again. At this stage, they should be able to:
- say times when they appear on the screen
- give the names of sports and hobbies as they appear on the screen
- use the vocabulary given in the programme for playing games in classroom activities
- use the greetings heard in both Programmes 1 and 2 in the classroom.

Arbeitsbogen 1

Name ....

Datum ....

Aufgabe 1

Wieviel Uhr ist es? Füll die Uhren aus.

What time is it? Put the time on these clocks:

Es ist acht Uhr

Es ist elf Uhr

Es ist drei Uhr

Es ist zehn Uhr

Es ist Mittag

Es ist sechs Uhr

Aufgabe 2

Füll die Zeichnungen und die Uhren aus.

Complete these drawings and fill in the times.

Es ist .... Uhr.

Ich spiele Tennis.

Es ist .... Uhr.

Ich sehe fern.

Es ist .... Uhr.

Ich tanze.

Es ist .... Uhr.

Ich laufe Schlittschuh.

Challenge: use your class library to find out at what time school starts and ends in German schools; at what time the evening news is on TV; at what time football matches start.

Arbeitsbogen 2

Name ....

Datum ....

Aufgabe 1
Was sind deine Hobbys?
What are your hobbies?
Hier ist Martins Tagebuch.
Was macht er jeden Tag nach der Schule?
Here is Martin's diary.
What does he plan to do after school for each day?

The Italian city Milan is called 'Mailand' in German.

Jetzt bist du dran. Was möchtest du machen? Und wann? Schreib dein eigenes Tagebuch.
Now it's your turn. What would you like to do? And when? Write your own diary.

Montag
Musik hören und Hausaufgaben machen

Dienstag
fernsehen – einen Film mit Arnold Schwarzenegger

Mittwoch
Rad fahren mit Andreas und Michelle

Donnerstag
mit Michelle ins Kino gehen

Freitag
bei McDonalds essen

Samstag
fernsehen – Fußball – AC Mailand mit Oliver Bierhoff – prima!

Sonntag
Hausaufgaben und lesen – Harry Potter – toll!

Aufgabe 2
Gruppenarbeit: Habt ihr diese Hobbys? Sprecht miteinander darüber!
Group activity: do you have these hobbies? Discuss them together.

Beispiel:
Example:

Eine Person sagt:
One of you says: Ich lese gern.

Die anderen sagen:
The others give an opinion:
Ja, toll! Ich lese auch gern!
Nein. Ich lese nicht gern.

Internet Challenge: what do young people like to watch on TV in Germany? And which films are they going to see? Find the TV programmes and films listed on the Internet. How many titles can you recognise?

Arbeitsbogen 3

Name ....

Datum ....

Aufgabe 1

Helmut treibt gern Sport. Er ist Sportfan! Am Sonntag treibt er von morgens bis abends Sport! Welcher Sport passt zu jeder Uhrzeit?

Here's Helmut the sports fan. On a Sunday, he plays sports from morning till night. Match the sport with the time.

Ich spiele Tennis ....um zehn Uhr..........

Ich spiele Fußball ....

Ich fahre Skateboard ....

Ich spiele Rugby ....

Ich schwimme ....

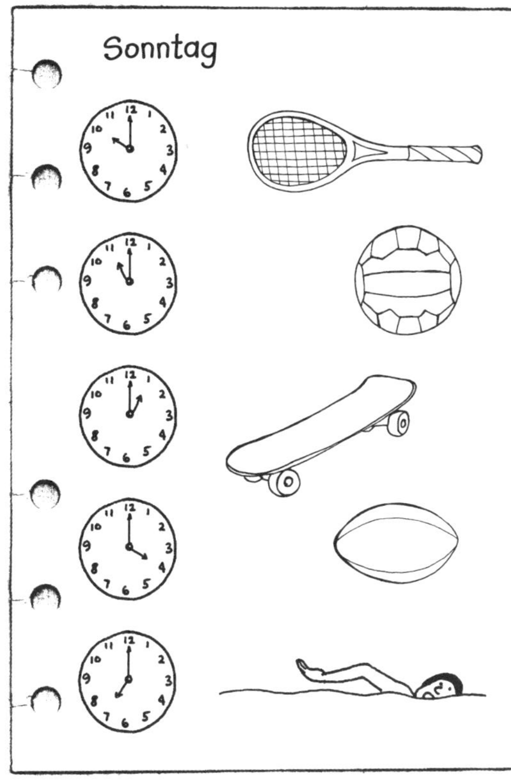

Aufgabe 2

Färbe diese Bilder und dann schneide sie aus, um Karten zu machen.

Colour in these drawings and then cut them up to make a set of cards.

Jetzt kannst du spielen.

Play some games using the cards: • Snap • Kim's game • find the pairs • memory

Aufgabe 3

Umfrage: Frag deine Klassenkameraden was für Sport sie gern treiben.

Carry out a survey of the people in your class. Ask what sports they like.

Beispiel: *Example:*

Schwimmst du gern?

Do you like swimming?

When you have their answers, make up a wall display showing what you have found out. You can have drawings and graphs showing how popular each sport is.

Arbeitsbogen 4

Name ....

Datum ....

Aufgabe 1

Spiel: Wer will Millionär sein?

Play: Who Wants to Be a Millionaire?

Make up a quiz about Germany. Each group in the class should put in five questions on topics such as:

- *countries where German is spoken*
- *German money*
- *famous Germans*
- *the names of cities in Germany, Austria and Switzerland*
- *German food and drink*

Then set up Who Wants to Be a Millionaire, with chairs, a host, contestants, an audience and friends to phone.

You can start with easy questions where the answers are only 'falsch' or 'richtig' and then have questions with a choice of four answers. Remember to have your prize money in marks.

Aufgabe 2

Zeichne dein eigenes Brettspiel mit 32 Kästchen.

Design your own board game. It should have 32 squares. Eight of the squares should have colours on them. Anyone who lands there should say the colour in German. Another eight squares should have questions on them about German. Here are some questions you could have about German:

- *what is the German word for 'I'?*
- *How do you spell 'elf'?*
- *How do you say 'I live in Scotland'?*

Another eight questions should be about German-speaking countries.

The last eight questions should be really difficult:

- *count from 20 to 1 in German*
- *name eight colours*
- *say your name, age and where you live in twenty seconds*

Arbeitsbogen 5

Name ....

Datum ....

Aufgabe 1

Lies das Tagebuch von Bayern-München und beantworte die Fragen.

Read this week's diary from the Bayern-München FC official website and answer the questions at the end.

1 On which days do the players train? ....

....

2 How many press conferences are there on Friday? ....

And on Tuesday? ....

3 On which days are they playing in the national league?

....

4 Who are they playing against?

....

DIE BAYERN-WOCHE

Montag, 04.09.
10.00 Uhr Training
ab 11.30 Uhr Pressekonferenz

Dienstag, 05.09.
12.15 Uhr Pressekonferenz
15.30 Uhr Pressekonferenz

Mittwoch, 06.09.
20.15 Uhr, 3. Bundesliga-Spieltag:
FC Bayern – VfL Wolfsburg
(live auf Premiere World)

Donnerstag, 07.09.
10.00 Uhr Training
ab 11.30 Uhr Pressekonferenz

Freitag, 08.09.
10.00 Uhr Pressekonferenz
17.00 Uhr Abschlusstraining in Stuttgart

Samstag, 09.09.
15.30 Uhr, 4. Bundesliga-Spieltag:
VfB Stuttgart – FC Bayern
(live auf Premiere World)

Sonntag, 10.09.
10.00 Uhr Training

Aufgabe 2

Schreib ein Tagebuch (von Montag bis Sonntag) für deine(n) Lieblingsmannschaft, Lieblingssportler(in) oder Lieblingssänger(in).

Make up a one-week diary for the team you support, for your favourite sports personality, or for your favourite singer.

Der falsche Rucksack!

The story

The children encourage Henning to improve his image by buying new clothes. Henning sets them the challenge of preparing for a picnic. Someone takes their rucksack by mistake and they have to seach for it all over town.They manage to find it and can finally enjoy their picnic.

Learning outcomes

This programme introduces pupils to:

- weather phrases
- words for travel and transport
- clothes
- picnic and recipe foods

They will also learn to recognise different parts of the verb sein, more verbs that follow the ich -e (ich wohne), du -st (du wohnst) pattern and some plurals of nouns.

Key vocabulary

- Clothes:
  die Kleider ▪ die Jeans ▪ das T-Shirt
  die Baseballmütze ▪ der Pulli ▪ die Hose ▪ die Socken
  die Jacke ▪ der Anorak ▪ die Schuhe ▪ der Stiefel
  der Schal ▪ der Badeanzug ▪ die Badehose
- Food:
  der Schinken ▪ die Eier ▪ die Brote ▪ die Tomaten
  die Gurke ▪ der Apfelsaft ▪ das Wasser ▪ die Cola
  die Schokolade
- Weather:
  es regnet ▪ es ist windig ▪ sonnig ▪ kalt ▪ heiß
  es schneit
- Travel/transport:
  das Auto ▪ die Strassenbahn ▪ der Bus ▪ der Zug
- Exclamations:
  schick! ▪ cool! ▪ zeig! ▪ bis später!
- Adjectives:
  alt ▪ neu ▪ kaputt

Before viewing

- The children should be introduced to a range of words for clothes. They can be told that Henning's clothes are – as he says – alt und kaputt – and they should bring from home a collection of clothes that might look like his. The children should practise saying the names in German with the teacher. The clothes can then be used in team games (preferably in the gym!) when pupils race each other to get to an item of clothing the teacher asks for in German and put it on. Thereafter, the clothes should be put up on a wall display and labelled with their German names.

- The pupils should also be told that Henning and the children will be going on a picnic. They can be set a dictionary challenge to find the longest list of words for picnic food in German in 20 minutes. The list can be collated and empty packaging of the top 15–20 items brought in for pupils to display and practise asking for.

- It is also worth introducing pupils to the words for transport at this stage.
  Flashcards will be needed, and pupils should practise saying 'ich fahre mit dem Zug', etc.

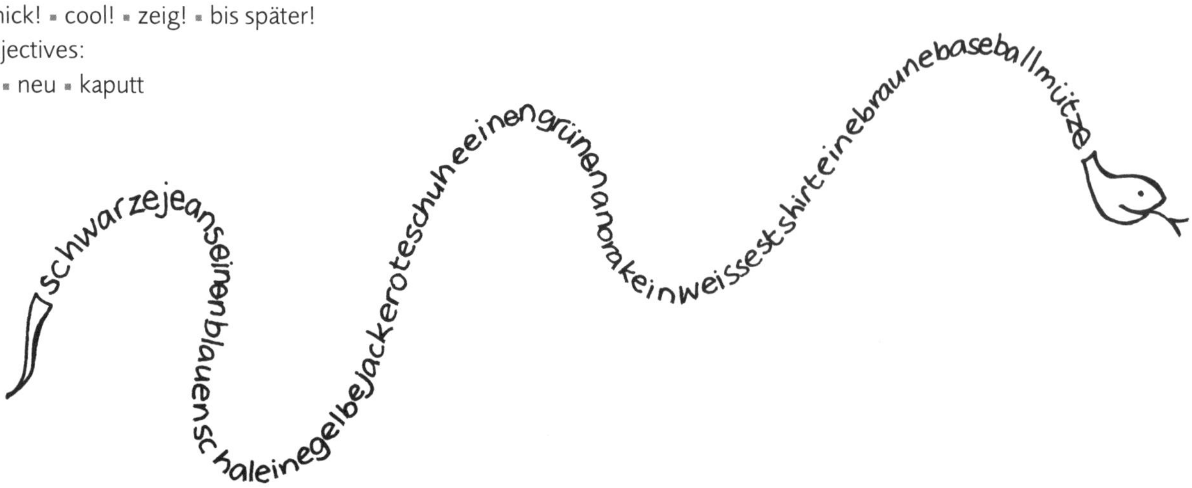

Language and culture

- Pupils should be set the task of finding out ten things about travel and transport in Germany: eg the Germans drive on the right; they are much stricter about rules, such as where you can cross the road; they drive very fast on motorways.

- Those pupils who are interested can also be given the task of finding out about the German Autobahn, about German cars and about German public transport.

During viewing

- Pupils can be asked to note whether the clothes Henning is wearing are anything like the clothes they brought in. They can watch the first part of the programme, and with colouring pens and pencils colour in the clothes he is wearing on a copy of the cut-out picture of him provided on page 40. They can then do Worksheet 1.

- Pupils should then watch the second part of the programme and draw the variety of food and drink the children are taking with them for their picnic. Pupils can then do Worksheet 2.

- After the next section of the programme they should complete Worksheet 3.

- The next section can be followed; Worksheet 4 and Worksheet 5 can be done at any time.

After viewing

- Pupils can expand their vocabulary of food and drink by planning in groups: the menu for a birthday party, a Christmas dinner, a meal in a fast food restaurant, etc.

- They should watch the programme again without pauses and practise saying the items of clothing, food and drink that they see.

- Have a class party. Each child – and the teacher – should provide something to eat or drink of German, Austrian or Swiss origin. Children could also try to make something German for the party from a recipe.

Name ....

Arbeitsbogen 1

Datum ....

Aufgabe 1

Wortschlange. Kannst du die Farben und die Kleider finden?

Word snake. Can you find the colours and the clothes?

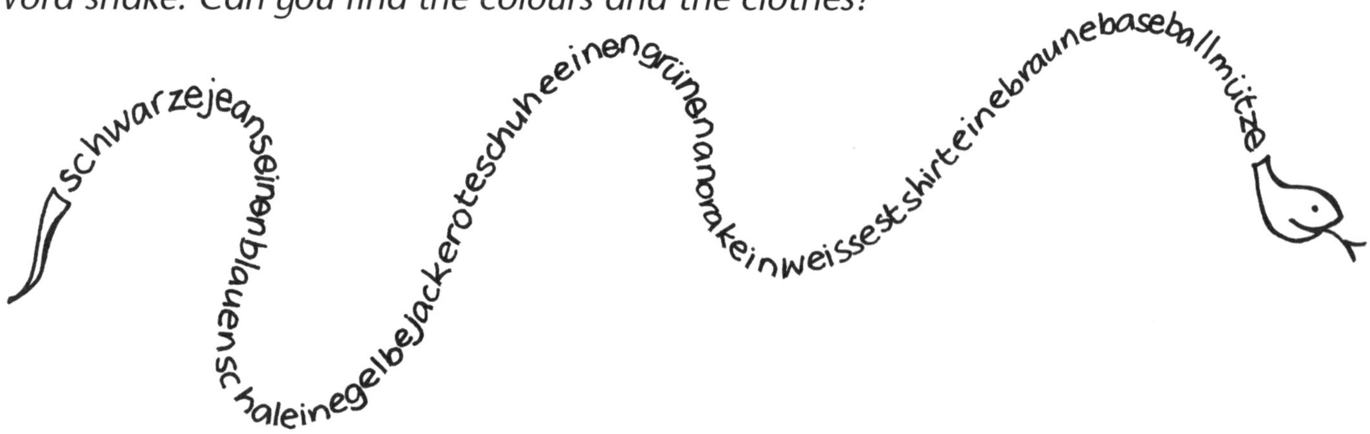

Schreib deine eigene Wortschlange!

Write your own word snake!

Aufgabe 2

Wie ist das Wetter? Was trägst du? Schreib die passenden Wörter.

What's the weather like? What do you wear? Match the clothes to the weather.

Es ist kalt. Ich trage...

Es ist heiß. Ich trage...

Es ist windig. Ich trage...

Es regnet. Ich trage...

eine warme Jacke
Sandalen
einen Schal
Stiefel
Shorts
meinen Anorak
einen Pullover
eine Mütze
ein T-Shirt

Internet challenge: find a German chat room from Yahoo! Deutschland (or another search engine of your choice) and find out what young people in German-speaking countries wear to school. Jeans and t-shirt? Uniform? (Vorsicht! Remember you never give out your full name or address on the Internet)

Arbeitsbogen 2

Name ....

Datum ....

Aufgabe 1

Unterstreiche in jeder Gruppe das nicht dazugehörige Wort.
Underline the 'odd word out' in each group.

1	Bananen	Äpfel	Käse	Orangen
2	Gurke	Eier	Bohnen	Salat
3	Tomaten	Cola	Wasser	Apfelsaft
4	Schinken	Käse	Milch	Butter
5	Bratwurst	Brot	Frikadellen	Schaschlik
6	Tee	Kaffee	Kakao	Limonade
7	Tomaten	Käse	Pizza	Oliven

Aufgabe 2

Rate zuerst was dein(e) Partner(in) gern oder nicht gern isst oder trinkt.
Dann stelle ihm/ihr die Fragen : Isst du gern…? Trinkst du gern…?
Guess first if your partner likes to eat and drink these foods. Then ask him or her and check your answers.

	Ich rate... ✓	Ich rate... ✗	Er/sie antwortet... ✓	Er/sie antwortet... ✗
Eier				
Hamburger				
Pizza				
Tomatensuppe				
Gurke				
Cola				
Apfelsaft				
Bananen				
Tee				

Aufgabe 3

Was isst Dracula gern? Blutwurst ?
What does Dracula like to eat? Black pudding? (Blutwurst is made with blood!)
Now what would you buy for a picnic with Rotkäppchen, Harry Potter, Prinz William, Bart Simpson, Dumbo …? Use the dictionary to find any types of food that you want to learn.

Arbeitsbogen 3

Name ....

Datum ....

Aufgabe 1

Wie fahren die Kinder? Was sagen sie?

How are the children travelling? What do they say?

Beispiel : Maria und Helmut sagen : „Wir fahren mit dem Zug."

Aufgabe 2

Stimmt das? Oder stimmt das nicht? Wenn ja, zeichne ein frohes Gesicht, wenn nein, zeichne ein trauriges Gesicht.

Are the sentences right, or not? If the sentence makes sense, draw a happy face. 
If not, draw a sad face. 

Die Kinder fahren mit der Strassenbahn zum Schwimmbad.

Die Kinder fahren mit dem Bus zum Stadion.

Am Fluss finden die Kinder ein Auto.

Mit dem Bus fahren ist schneller als mit dem Skateboard.

Wir fahren mit dem Zug nach Amerika.

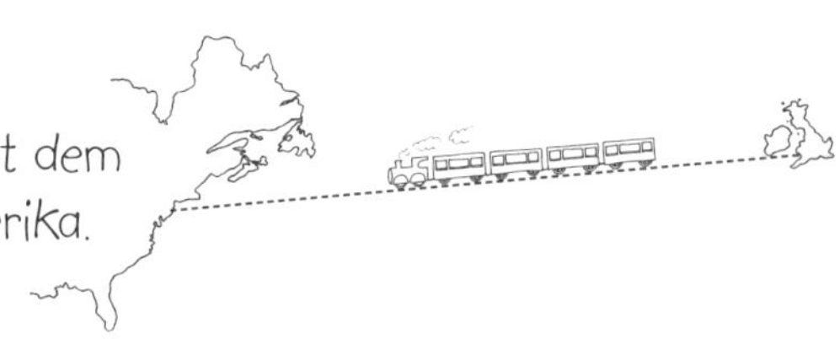

Aufgabe 3

Umfrage: Was für Autos haben deine Lehrer(innen)/Hilfslehrer(innen)/Eltern? Füll die Tabelle aus.

What kind of cars do your teachers /school helpers/ parents have? Complete the table.

	Name	Was für ein Auto hat er/sie?	Aus welchem Land kommt es?	Welche Farbe hat es?	Wie alt ist es?
Beispiel	Frau Braun	Mercedes	Deutschland	Blau	4 Jahre alt

Arbeitsbogen 4

Name ....

Datum ....

Aufgabe 1

Wie ist das Wetter? Kannst du das lesen? Welcher Satz passt zu welchem Bild?

What is the weather like? Can you read the sentences? Which sentence goes with each picture?

Es ist heiß

Es ist windig

Es regnet

Es schneit

Es ist kalt

....

Aufgabe 2

Wie ist das Wetter? Schreib die richtigen Sätze unter die Bilder.

What's the weather like? Write the correct sentences under each picture.

....

es regnet		Paris
es schneit		London
es ist heiß	in	New York
es ist windig		Venedig
es ist kalt		Pisa

Internet challenge: Use a German search engine (Yahoo! Deutschland, allesklar.de) to find out what the weather is like today in: Genf, Wien, München, Köln

What are these towns called in English? Choose a town in a German-speaking country and start a weather diary, comparing their weather with the weather in your area. You can check once a week or once a month.

Arbeitsbogen 5

Name ....

Datum ....

Aufgabe 1

Vier Kinder machen ein Picknick. Jedes Kind will sein eigenes Lieblingsessen und sein Lieblingsgetränk haben. Sie tragen alle verschiedene Kleider und Farben! Kannst du die Tabelle ausfüllen?

Four children are having a picnic. Each wants their favourite food and drink. They are all wearing different (and different coloured) clothes. Can you fill in the chart?

Lieblingsessen: Schinken, Eier, Tomaten, Bananen
Lieblingsgetränke: Mineralwasser, Cola, Milch, Apfelsaft
Lieblingsfarben: rot, gelb, braun, schwarz
Kleider: Pullover, Jeans, Hose, T-Shirt

	isst gern	trinkt gern	Lieblingsfarbe	trägt...
Anna				
Katrin				
Dieter				
Hans				

1. Dieter isst gern Schinken.
2. Annas Lieblingsfarbe ist rot.
3. Der Junge, der Milch trinkt, isst auch gern Eier.
4. Anna trinkt nicht gern Apfelsaft.
5. Der Pullover ist rot.
6. Katrins Lieblingsgetränk ist Apfelsaft.
7. Ein Mädchen trägt Jeans.
8. Annas Lieblingsessen hat dieselbe Farbe wie ihre Kleider!
9. Katrin isst kein Fleisch.
10. Hans trägt eine braune Hose.
11. Katrins Lieblingsessen ist gelb, und ihre Lieblingsfarbe auch.
12. Dieter trägt nicht gern einen Pullover.
13. Das Mädchen, das Cola trinkt, trägt nie schwarz.

Aufgabe 2

Schreib deinen eigenen Kleider – oder Essenskatalog. Du findest Fotos in alten Zeitschriften.

Make your own catalogue of clothes or foods. You'll find photos in old magazines.

Internet challenge: What are German young people wearing? Do the clothes cost more or less than here? And what about food? Find some German shopping sites and compare what you find.

So ein Lärm!

The story

Fed up with the children disturbing him, Henning sets them a seemingly impossible challenge; to find a really scary looking animal which makes a horrible sound. The search ends when the children discover the statue of the Musicians of Bremen and we see and hear the story acted.

Learning outcomes

This programme introduces pupils to:

- pets and other animals
- the noises that animals make

They will also learn to recognise the plurals of some present tense verbs and the er/sie/es part singular of some present tense verbs.

Key vocabulary

- Pets:
  der Hund ▪ die Katze ▪ das Pferd ▪ der Goldfisch
  der Hamster
- Other animals:
  der Esel ▪ der Hahn ▪ die Kuh ▪ das Schwein
  der Löwe ▪ der Tiger ▪ der Elefant ▪ der Wellensittich
- Places animals are kept:
  der Zoo ▪ die Tierhandlung ▪ der Bauernhof

Before viewing

- Tell pupils the title of the programme and the subject of the key vocabulary: pets, animals and the noises they make. After discussion, ask everyone to write down what they think the programme is going to be about. Pin the ideas up on the wall.

- Get the children to make flashcards of the animals listed under 'Key vocabulary' and use the cards to teach their names in German.

- You can use the following information to start the class on a search for information on animal noises:

> **Language and culture**
> As you would expect, animals make different sounds in German, just as people do. Here are a few examples:
> Vögel: tswit, tswit
> Katzen: miau, miau
> Kühe: mmuuh
> Hund: wau wau
> Esel: iaah, iaah
> Frösche: quaak, quaak
> Wölfe: huh
> Hühner, Hennen: gak, gak
> Mäuse: piep, piep
> Schlangen: sss
>
> You can find more of this on the Internet at http://www.georgetown.edu/cball/animals/german.html

During viewing

- Watch the first section of the programme. Pupils should be able to follow easily. Ask them to do Worksheet 1.

- Worksheet 4 is for revision and consolidation and can be done at any time. Give the children a copy of the resource sheet on page 39 to use with exercise 1.

- After watching the second section of the programme, check with the class that they have been following what Henning is up to. Let them do Worksheet 2.

- During the third section, the pupils should join in the guessing game, naming the animals the children on screen are imitating.

- The pupils should watch the fourth section of the programme as often as necessary and then work out with you how they would present their pet:
  Ich habe **einen** Hund. **Er** heißt Rex. (masculine)
  Ich habe **eine** Katze. **Sie** heißt Mitzi. (feminine)

- Check that the children understand the difference between the masculine and feminine forms. Then get them to introduce their own pets, using photographs brought from home.

- The final section, the Bremen Town Band, should be watched several times over and discussed with the class using these websites:
  - the story of the Musicians of Bremen in English: http://www.pitt.edu/~dash/type0130.html#bremen
  - the same story in German: hhttp://gutenberg.aol.de/grimm/maerchen/stadtmu1.htm

  The children can then do Worksheet 5.

- If you want to know more about the Grimm Brothers who first wrote down this story and many others, have a look at: http://www.pitt.edu/~dash/grimm.html#chronology

After viewing

- Check if anyone guessed correctly what the theme of the programme was going to be.

- Get the class to do Worksheet 3. They can use a copy of the game board on page 42 as an alternative to creating their own board.
  Divide the children into groups of four and give them some time to work on one of the following collages:
  - a Noah's Ark – die Arche Noah – with a range of animals going in
  - Old MacDonald's Farm – der Bauernhof vom alten MacDonald
  - (if it's close to Christmas) a Nativity scene with lots of animals around the crib.

- One group could also prepare a parade of the class's favourite mascots and soft toys brought in from home.

- Let the children take time to present what they have made: Hier ist McDonalds Bauernhof und hier sind die Tiere: der Elefant, etc.

- You may wish to follow up the story of the Bremen Town Band by introducing other stories by the Grimm Brothers; some pupils may not have heard of them.

- If the children wish to write to the tourist office in Bremen for information, you may wish to use this format:

```
In unserer Klasse studieren wir
die Stadt Bremen und möchten
uns darüber informieren.

Könnten Sie uns bitte etwas
über die Stadt schreiben?

Mit freundlichen Grüssen

      [signature]
```

Arbeitsbogen 1

Name ....

Datum ....

Aufgabe 1

Wähl die passenden Namen für die Tierteile.

Match the animal parts to their names in German:

eg 1 - das Zebra

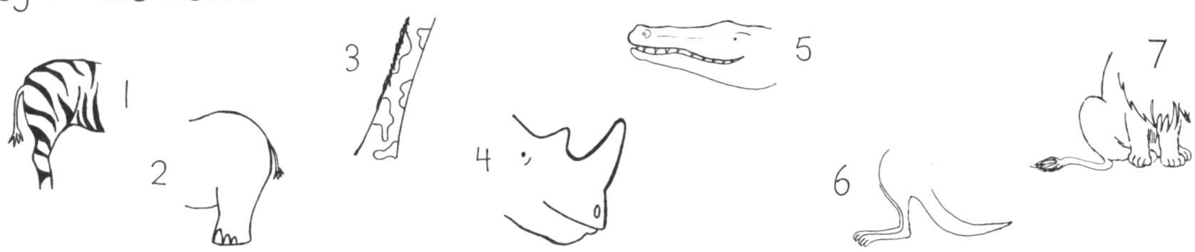

das Känguruh

die Giraffe

das Krokodil

der Elefant

das Nashorn

der Löwe

das Zebra

Aufgabe 2

Zeichne einen Pfeil, um die Tiere in ihr Zuhause zu bringen.

Draw an arrow to put the animals in their homes.

Dictionary challenge: what's your favourite animal? Write out its name in German and look in the dictionary for adjectives that describe the animal and fit the name.

Mein	sc**H**ön	**Meine**	**K**omisch
	fre**U**ndlich		**A**ktiv
	liebe**N**swert		**T**reu
	Dumm		**Z**ahm
			intellig**E**nt

Internet challenge: go back to the website http://sps.k12.mo.us/khs/german/gerlinks.htm where you found German coats of arms and find out: how many states have an animal on their coat of arms – and what is the animal called in German?

Arbeitsbogen 2

Name ....

Datum ....

Aufgabe 1

Bremen – *Internet challenge*

You can find a lot of information about Bremen just by going to three Internet sites:

http://www.bremen.de/info/bremen/Willkommene.html

http://member.aol.com/highsky767/html/tour.html

http://www.bremen-tourism.de/english/frame-expo-neu.htm

Have a virtual tour of Bremen on these sites and then see if you can find out:

1 What can you do in Bremen if you like sport?

2 What is the Rathaus – and are cars allowed in the square in front?

3 When is the Bremen music festival held?

4 What is the Neptunbrunnen?

5 What is the Schulschiff Deutschland?

6 What is SV Werder?

7 What happens at Bremerhaven?

8 Is there an airport in Bremen?

Make a factfile about Bremen and put it up so people can see:

- *how many people live there*
- *what the shops are like*
- *whether they have good clubs and cafés*
- *what people do for a living*
- *what their houses are like*
- *how many schools there are.*

Aufgabe 2

Pick one aspect of life in Bremen that you would like to study and make a scrapbook or a wall display about it.

You could study entertainment in Bremen and find out:

- *how many cinemas there are*
- *what films are on at the moment (are there any with titles you recognise?)*
- *what time they start*
- *how much it costs to get in.*

Challenge: make up a presentation about the aspect of life in Bremen you have studied and tell your group all about it.

Arbeitsbogen 3

Name ....

Datum ....

Aufgabe 1

Spiel dieses Brettspiel.
Du brauchst einen Würfel.
Play a game of Snakes and Ladders, using the board opposite and a dice.

Make a board like the one on the right. If you land on a box showing a part of the body and a ladder, you have to say the name in German so that you can go up the ladder: for example, legs – Beine.

If you land on a snake, you can avoid going down by saying in German the word for the picture on that square. You also have to give the name for another drawing, but your partner gets to choose the picture square!

The first person to get from square 1 to square 36 is the winner!

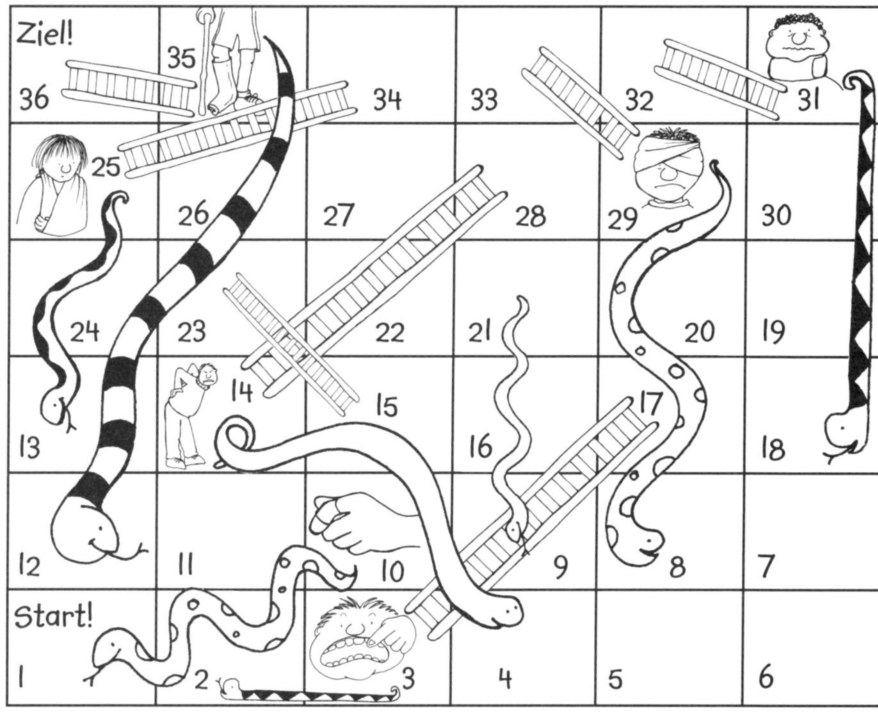

Aufgabe 2

Zeichne ein Ungeheuer. Arbeite mit drei Klassenkameraden zusammen.
Draw a monster. Work in a group of three.

You will each need pieces of paper, some with colours written on them and some with parts of the body written on them. You will also need paper to draw on and colouring pens or pencils.

Put the two piles of paper face down on the table. Take it in turns to turn over a colour and a part of the body and tell the rest of the group what to draw and what colour to make it: der Kopf ist grün

Everyone should then draw a head and colour it green.

Now put your drawings up on the wall and write a sentence in German next to each one describing what it is like, for example: die Augen sind gelb.

der Körper	ist	rot
das Haar		schwarz-grau
die Arme	sind	blau
die Beine		grün
die Augen		weiß-gelb

Challenge! Tongue twisters – Zungenbrecher: how fast can you say these phrases? Time each other:

In Ulm und um Ulm und um Ulm herum.
Fischers Fritz fischt frische Fische. Frische Fische fischt Fischers Fritz.
Es klapperten die Klapperschlangen bis die Klappern schlapper klangen.
Wir Wiener Waschweiber würden weiße Wäsche waschen, Wenn wir wüssten, wo warmes Wasser wäre.
Weiß Werner, wie wenig die Violetten in der Valentinsvase wiegen?
Ob er aber über Oberammergau Oder ob er über Unterammergau Oder ob er überhaupt nicht kommt, ist nicht gewiss.
Brautkleid bleibt Brautkleid, und Blaukraut bleibt Blaukraut.

Arbeitsbogen 4

Name ....

Datum ....

Aufgabe 1

Mache einige dieser Fünf-Minuten-Spiele:

Do some of these 5-minute activities:

- *Make up a wordsearch with five colours, five parts of the body, five animals and five boys' names*
- *Play a game of lotto with the names of animals or clothes or colours*
- *Make up a crossword where all the clues are ways to travel*
- *Make up an odd-one-out quiz: blau neun rot grün and get someone in your group to do it*

Use the drawing of Henning's house to keep a note of your scores: every time you win a game, you get to colour in another part of the house. The champion will be the person with the whole house coloured in!

Finally, here's an activity that will take a little longer: make a weather circle to sit on your desk. Write the German weather sentences on the back.

Aufgabe 2

Male den Clown an. Die Rechenaufgaben werden dir helfen, sein Gesicht und seine Kleider anzumalen.

Colour in the clown. When you've done the sums, you'll know what colours to make his face and clothes.

10 blau
50 orange
20 gelb
60 grün
30 rot
70 grau
40 weiß
80 schwarz

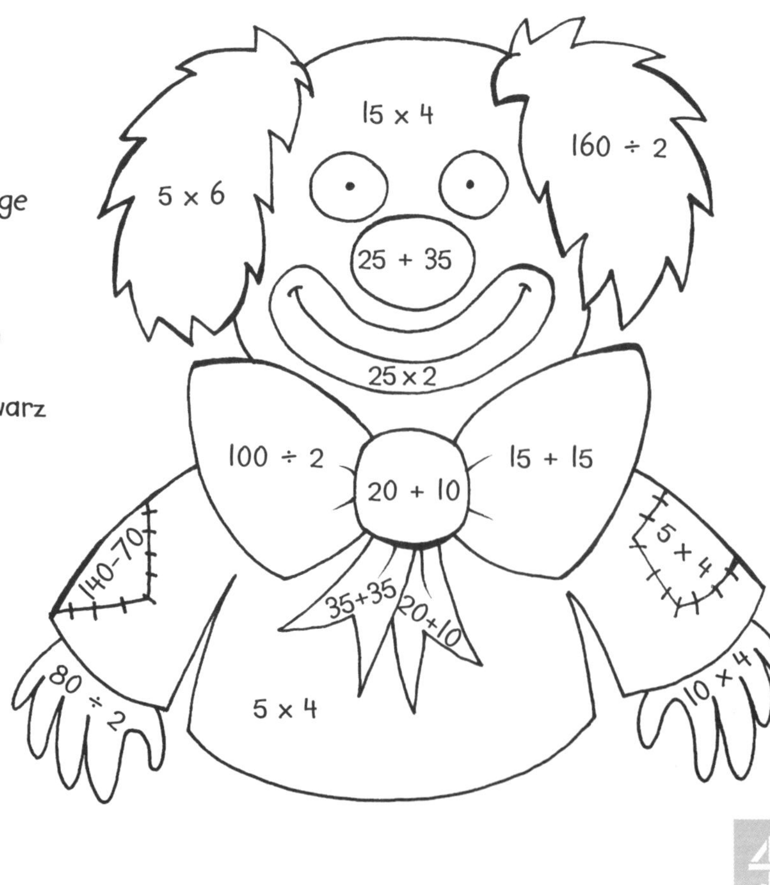

Arbeitsbogen 5

Name ....

Datum ....

Aufgabe 1

Umfrage

Frag deine Klassenkameraden was für Haustiere sie haben.

Conduct a survey to find out what pets the people in your class have.

Then make up a bar chart or a pie chart to show how many people have no pet, how many have a dog, etc.

Frag deine Klassenkameraden :

Was für ein Haustier hast du?	
Ich habe	eine Katze einen Hamster einen Fisch ein Pferd eine Schlange ein Meerschweinchen einen Wellensittich ein Kaninchen kein Haustier

Aufgabe 2

Spiel

You will need a counter to do this activity. Draw animals like the ones below on a piece of paper. Throw the counter and say the name of the animal the counter lands on – then make the noise it makes.

Aufgabe 3

Lies die Geschichte der Bremer Stadtmusikanten, und dann zeichne deinen eigenen Cartoon.

Read the story of the Bremen Town Band and then turn it into a cartoon.

Das sind die Tiere.	Sie gehen nach Bremen. Sie haben Hunger.	Im Haus sind Räuber. Sie haben viel Essen.
Die Tiere machen schrecklichen Lärm.	Die Räuber haben Angst. Sie rennen weg.	Die Tiere essen. Sie sind froh.

Make the cartoon into a play for your group. Make masks for the animals and the robbers. Give each person a part to act out and have one person to tell the story. Video your story or act it out for a younger class or at assembly and see how well other people can understand your German.

Hennings Geburtstag

The story

The children face two challenges: to find out Henning's age and to shop for his party. After the celebration, Henning's train moves away to an unknown destination.

Learning outcomes

This programme introduces pupils to:

- days and birthday dates
- family members
- handling money
- organising a party – food and drink, shops
- numbers above 20

They will also learn to recognise the present tense of haben.

Key vocabulary

- Days:
  Montag ▪ Dienstag ▪ Mittwoch ▪ Donnerstag
  Freitag ▪ Samstag ▪ Sonntag
  ich habe am .... Geburtstag
- Months:
  Januar ▪ Februar ▪ März ▪ April ▪ Mai ▪ Juni ▪ Juli
  August ▪ September ▪ Oktober ▪ November ▪ Dezember
- Family:
  eine Schwester ▪ ein Bruder ▪ die Mutter ▪ der Vater
  der Großvater ▪ die Großmutter
- Food and drink:
  die Tomaten ▪ die Gurke ▪ der Salat ▪ das Mehl
  die Eier ▪ die Butter ▪ die Milch ▪ die Schokolade
  der Käse ▪ die Wurst ▪ das Brot
- Shops:
  auf dem Markt ▪ im Supermarkt ▪ in der Bäckerei
- Verbs:
  third person plural: sie essen ▪ sie trinken ▪ sie spielen

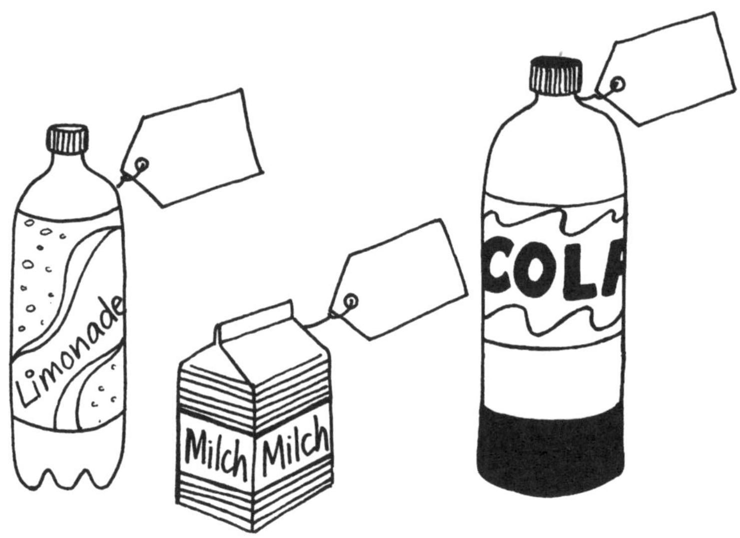

Before viewing

- ☐ Teach the days of the week and the months and get the class to make them into raps which they can recite every day, like the rap they hear in each programme.
- ☐ Ask the class to make desk calendars and have them display and say the day and date every day.
- ☐ Make a wall calendar of all their birthdays – and yours! – and celebrate the birthdays by putting up a birthday 'train' (see page 43).
- ☐ Put out a display of plastic food and drink packaging, and label the items in German. Teach pupils to ask for the items, saying for example 'Ich möchte Schokolade, bitte'. They should also get to know: 'Danke' and 'Bitte schön'.

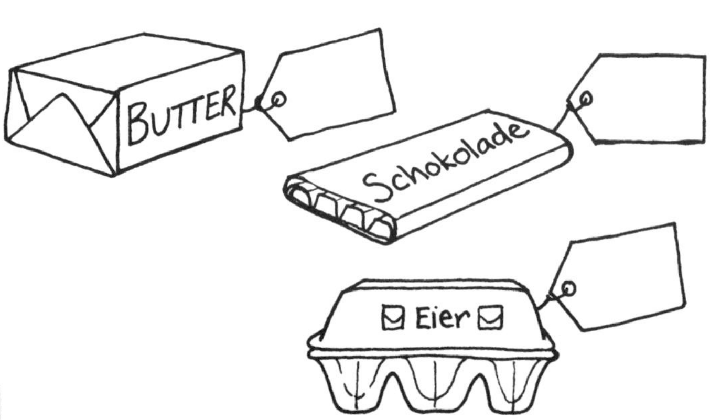

Language and culture

- Set pupils the challenge of finding out about shopping in Germany. They should try to discover when shops are open and – very important from the point of view of tourists – which days of the week shops close.

- This would also be a good time for them to find out about the German approach to recycling, with different bins in every household for glass, plastic, etc. There are also strict rules for packaging that make the manufacturer pay if too much is used.

During viewing

- The class should watch the first part of the programme, reciting with the children and Henning any language they recognise, such as the days. They can then do Worksheet 1.

- The class should watch the next section – about birthdays – stopping the video as they hear each person say their age and birthday. They should then say their own age and birthday. They can then do Worksheet 2.

- The third section of the programme contains the challenge Henning sets the children. You should make a copy of the riddle for the wall and let pupils discuss it. When they have heard and seen the quest, ask pupils to make a classroom display of the places the children visit and the foods they get there. Pupils can then do Worksheet 3.

- The fourth section of the programme shows the children preparing the birthday meal. The class should try reading recipes in German and should read English language recipe books for recipes originating in Germany which they can try out at home. They can then do Worksheet 4.

- Pupils should watch the last part of the programme and then make birthday cards in German, with German greetings for Henning. They can then do Worksheet 5.

After viewing

- After watching the programme in sections, you should then let the children watch it straight through and contribute as much as they can of the language. They should now be able to make up with your help a profile of Henning, with descriptions in German of:
  - his clothes and their colours
  - his age
  - the foods and drinks he likes
  - his hobbies
  - his house, etc.

- They can then make up a profile of themselves to take home as a record of all they have learned in German so far.

- The birthday train: the birthday girl's or boy's name is written in the smoke. Their age is written on the front and 'Herzlichen Glückwunsch' is written along the side of the train. The resource sheet on page 43 can be copied for this purpose.

Arbeitsbogen 1

Name ....

Datum ....

Aufgabe 1

Finde Bilder einer Familie aus deiner Lieblings-Soap oder deinem Lieblingsfilm.

Find pictures of a family from your favourite soap on television or your favourite film. Stick in the pictures or draw them and complete the sentences about each character. You may have to use your imagination for the ages and birthdays.

Hier ist der Vater. Er heißt .... Er ist .... Jahre alt. Er hat am .... Geburtstag.

Hier ist die Mutter. Sie heißt .... Sie ist .... Jahre alt. Sie hat am .... Geburtstag.

Hier ist der Sohn. Er heißt .... Er ist .... Jahre alt. Er hat am .... Geburtstag.

Hier ist die Tochter. Sie heißt .... Sie ist .... Jahre alt. Sie hat am .... Geburtstag.

Aufgabe 2

Partnerspiel: Wer bin ich?

Work with a partner: Who am I?

Choose a character from a TV programme or film. Your partner must try to guess which person you have chosen in ten questions or fewer. But they can only ask questions which can be answered by 'Ja' or 'Nein'. If you answer 'Das weiß ich nicht' the question does not count.

Beispiele:

Bist du ein Mann? Bist du eine Frau?

Bist du fünfzig Jahre alt? Bist du zehn Jahre alt?

Jünger? Älter?

Hast du eine Tochter? Hast du einen Sohn?

Wohnst du in England? Wohnst du in Deutschland?

Aufgabe 3

Wie alt sind sie?

How old are the members of this family?

Herr Braun, der Vater, ist zweiundzwanzig Jahre älter als seine Tochter, Sarah.

Herr Braun ist achtundzwanzig Jahre jünger als sein Vater, Sarahs Großvater.

Sarah ist zwei Jahre älter als ihr Bruder, Jan.

Niklas ist vier Jahre jünger als Sarah.

Niklas ist sechs Jahre alt.

Jans Mutter ist zweiundzwanzig Jahre älter als Jan.

Jan ist fünfzig Jahre jünger als seine Großmutter.

Herr Braun	Niklas	Jan	Sarah	Frau Braun	Großvater	Großmutter
....	....	....	....	....	....	....

Arbeitsbogen 2

Name ....

Datum ....

Aufgabe 1
Thomas hat dir eine E-mail geschrieben. Füll die Lücken im folgenden Text auf Englisch aus.
You have received an e-mail from Thomas in Germany telling you how he spends his birthday. Fill in the blanks in the English version that follows, so you can explain to your friends what he does.

> Am Dienstag habe ich Geburtstag! Ich bin elf Jahre alt! Meine Freunde Marcus und Holger kommen zu Besuch.
>
> Wenn das Wetter schön ist, machen wir ein Picknick im Garten – Cola, Limonade, belegte Brote, Schokolade und viele Bonbons. Alles was ich gern esse und trinke! Dann spielen wir Fußball.
>
> Wenn es regnet, machen wir das Picknick im Haus und wir spielen mit dem Computer.

His birthday is on .... day. He is .... years old. His friends .... and .... are coming to visit. If the weather is .... they will have a .... in the ...., with ...., ..., ..., ..., and lots of .... Everything he likes to eat and ....! Then they will play .... If it .... they will have the .... in the .... and play with the ....

Aufgabe 2
Was machst du, wenn du Geburtstag hast? Beschreibe das in ein paar Sätzen.
What do you do on your birthday? Write a few sentences in German in the form of a newspaper report. Here are some examples to start you off:

(your name) hat heute Geburtstag!

(your name) wird heute ....
Jahre alt. ....
.... und .... (your friends' names)
kommen zu Besuch.
Sie essen .... (foods) und trinken
.... (drinks).
Sie spielen .... (games)

Internet Challenge: what other events can you celebrate with „eine Party?" How do German-speaking people celebrate them? Use a chat room or an Internet search to find out.

Name ....

Arbeitsbogen 3

Datum ....

Aufgabe 1

Wir haben unsere Einkaufsliste zerrissen. Kannst du uns helfen, die Lücken auszufüllen?

We have torn our shopping list. Can you help us to fill in the blanks?

Aufgabe 2

Partnerspiel: Du zeichnest etwas zum Essen oder zum Trinken und schreibst wieviel das kostet. Dein(e) Partner(in) rät den Preis. Du antwortest nur „Mehr" oder „Weniger" bis er/sie es geschafft hat.

Partner game: Draw something to eat or drink. Label it with a price. Your partner tries to guess how much it costs, but you must only answer "more" or "less" until he/she gets it right.

Internet challenge: What money do they use in Germany? In Switzerland? In Austria? In Namibia? What do the words and pictures used on the notes and pictures tell you about the country? Make a wall display.

Arbeitsbogen 4

Name ....

Datum ....

Aufgabe 1

Hennings Geburtstagsmenü ist ein Geheimnis. Kannst du das Rätsel lösen?

Henning's birthday menu is a secret. Can you solve the puzzle?

A	Ä	B	C	D	E	F	G	H	I	J	K	L	M	N	O	P	Q	R	S	T	U	V	W	X	Y	Z
✌	⓪	👌	👍	👎	☜	☞	☝	☟	✋	☺	😐	☹	💣	☠	⚐	🏱	✈	☼	💧	❄	✞	✝	⌖	✠	✡	☪

Geburtstagsmenü

❄⚐💣✌❄☜☠💧✞🏱🏱☜

🏱✋☪☪✌ 💣✋❄ ❄⚐💣✌❄☜☠ ✞☠👎 ☝✞☼😐☜☠

👌☜☹☜☝❄☜ 👌☼⚐❄☜ 💣✋❄ ☹☜👌☜☼⌖✞☼💧❄

😐⓪💧☜ ✞☠👎 💧✌☹✌❄

☝☜👌✞☼❄💧❄✌☝💧😐✞👍☟☜☠

Aufgabe 2

Was brauchen wir, um Hennings Geburtstagskuchen zu machen? Füll die Lücken aus.

What do we need for Henning's birthday cake? Fill in the blanks.

Z __ __ __ __ __

E __ __ __

M __ __ __

K __ __ __ __ __

B __ __ __ __ __

S __ __ __ __ __ __ __ __ __

Challenge: Was isst man in Deutschland? Just as we have 'Yorkshire pudding' or 'Devon Teas', many parts of Germany and German-speaking countries have their own specialities. Find out in which areas Sauerkraut and Schwarzwälder Kirschtorte originated. Why not start your own German cook book? Or have a party with as many German ingredients as you can find in your local shops.

Arbeitsbogen 5

Name ....

Datum ....

Aufgabe 1

Gruppenspiel. Spielt in Gruppen von vier Personen.

Play in groups of four. Each person in turn throws a dice in order to decorate a pizza. For example: you throw a one – you can put on the cheese; you throw a two – you can put on the salami. Careful! You should only speak in German AND be polite. For example, ,,Ein eins! Käse, bitte!"

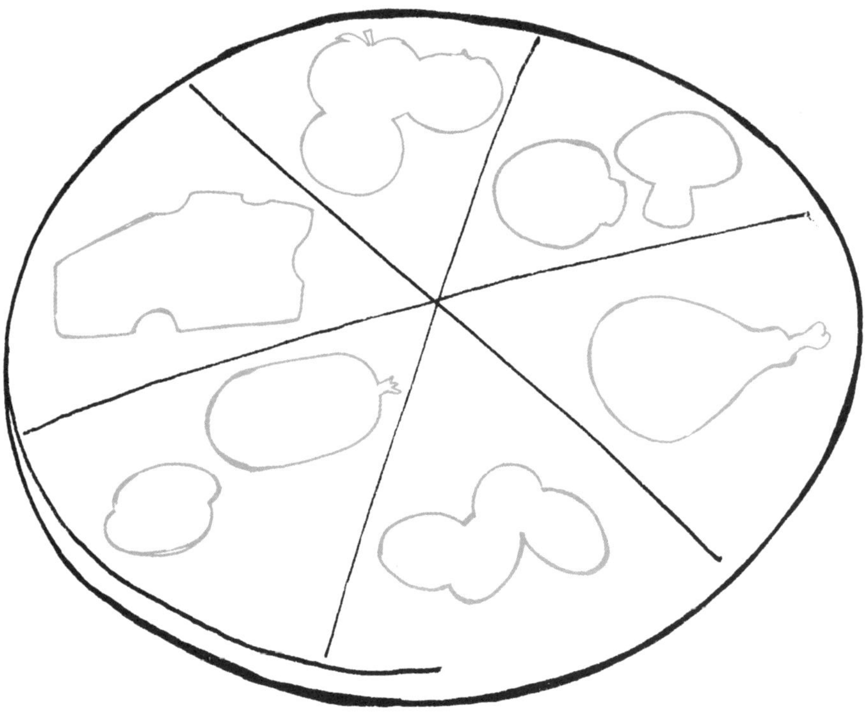

Aufgabe 2

Partnerspiel. Frage deinen Partner/deine Partnerin diese Zahlen ab. Du sagst EINE Zahl und dein(e) Partner(in) kringelt die richtige Zahl ein.

Test your partner with these sets of numbers. You say ONE of the three numbers and your partner circles the correct one:

5	14	1	78	50	19	6	10	2	2
15	40	11	87	60	29	16	100	3	200
50	400	21	870	70	39	60	20	9	2000

Internet Challenge: How many...?
Each answer is a number.
Wieviel(e)...?
... Stiefschwestern hatte Aschenputtel?
... Gipfel gibt es in Rom?
... Dalmatiner gab es?
... Zwerge gibt es in „Schneewittchen"?
... war MMM zu römischen Zeiten?
... Töchter hat Homer Simpson?
... Musiker haben bei den „Beatles" gespielt?
... Söhne hatte Wilhelm Tell?
... Kinder hatte Herr von Trapp?
... Soldaten hatte der Herzog von York?

Hennings Haus

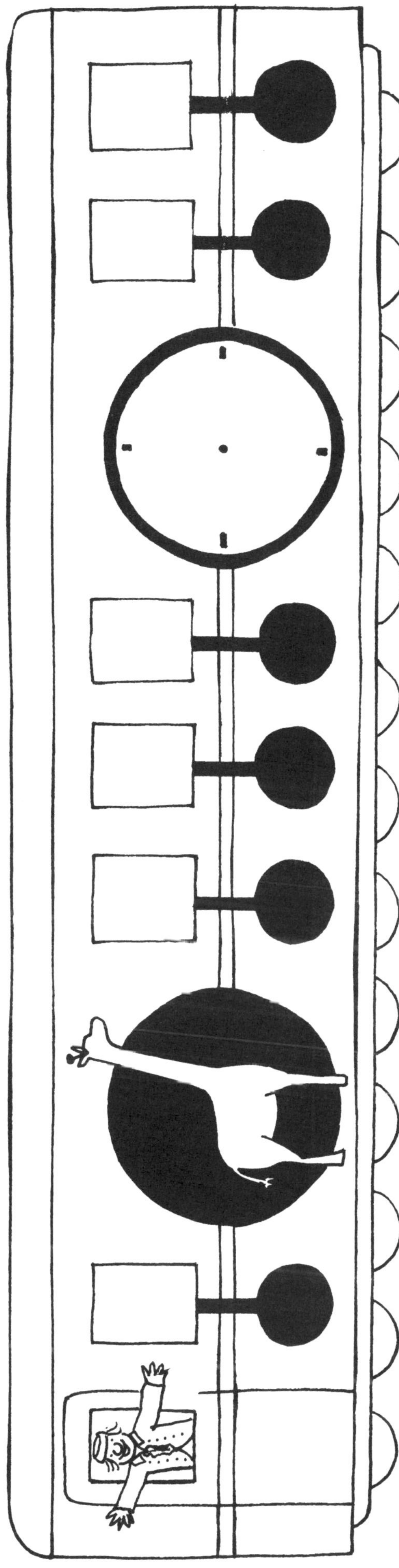

Henning

Deutschland

Brettspiel

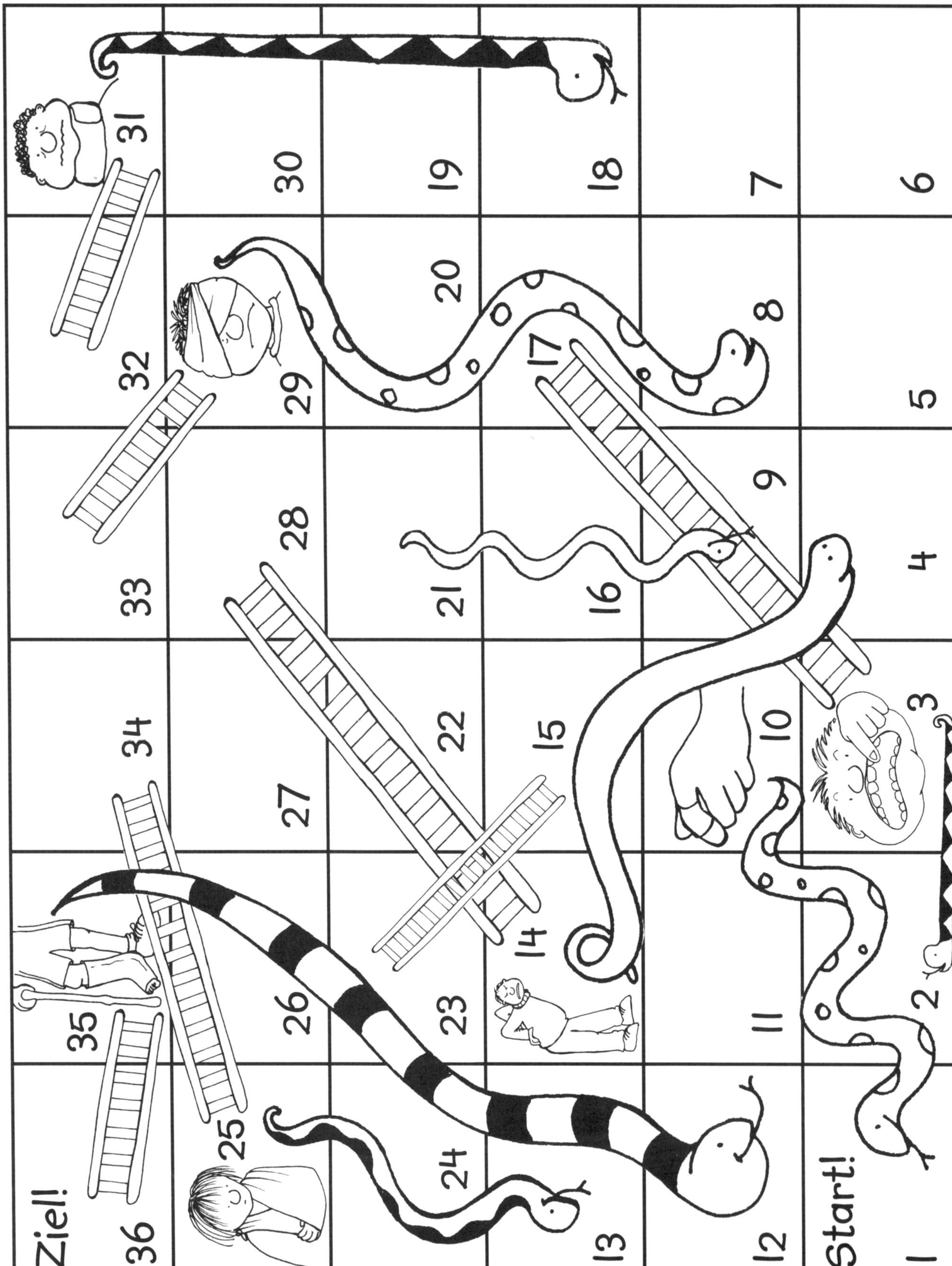

Start!
Ziel!
1
2
3
4
5
6
7
8
9
10
11
12
13
14
15
16
17
18
19
20
21
22
23
24
25
26
27
28
29
30
31
32
33
34
35
36

Herzlichen
Glückwunsch

Answer Sheet

Page 7
Aufgabe 3

B	A	D	E	N	S	C	H	H	W	I	G
W	Ü	R	T	T	E	M	B	E	R	G	R
S	V	K	H	S	A	Q	S	S	V	H	U
S	B	O	H	M	P	G	W	S	L	B	B
S	N	T	R	U	X	R	Y	E	O	O	N
A	G	S	F	P	J	U	I	N	R	R	E
A	E	A	B	D	O	B	K	J	S	Z	L
R	G	C	B	N	E	M	E	R	B	T	K
L	B	H	G	I	X	A	M	O	E	L	C
A	H	S	O	O	V	H	Z	E	Y	A	E
N	R	E	Y	A	B	H	R	E	R	H	M
D	I	N	U	E	B	E	R	L	I	N	I
N	I	E	H	R	D	R	O	N	W	A	Z
N	I	E	D	E	R	A	W	R	R	N-	N
Z	L	A	F	P	S	A	C	H	S	E	N
N	E	G	I	W	S	E	L	H	C	S	O
G	C	Ü	N	E	G	N	I	R	Ü	H	T
-D	N	A	L	N	I	E	H	R	E	C	Ü
H	W	E	S	T	F	A	L	E	N	A	N
H	O	L	S	T	E	I	N	E	N	S	W
B	R	A	N	D	E	N	B	U	R	G	Ü

Page 8
Aufgabe 2

Die Bananen sind gelb. Die Orangen sind orange. Die Erdbeeren sind rot. Die Bohnen sind grün. Die Weintrauben sind grün/schwarz.

Page 9
Aufgabe 1

Albert Einstein, Steffi Graf, Ludwig van Beethoven, Arnold Schwarzenegger, Oliver Bierhoff.

Aufgabe 3

Aschenputtel	Cinderella
Schneewittchen	Snow White
der Froschkönig	The Frog Prince
Dornröschen	Sleeping Beauty
der Rattenfänger von Hameln	The Pied Piper
Rotkäppchen	Little Red Riding Hood

Page 17
Aufgabe 1

(1) Monday, Thursday, Friday and Sunday
(2) One press conference on Friday, and two on Tuesday
(3) Wednesday and Saturday
(4) Wolfsburg and Stuttgart

Page 21
Aufgabe 1

(1) Käse (2) Eier (3) Tomaten (4) Schinken (5) Brot (6) Limonade (7) Pizza (the other foods are the ingredients, pizza is the dish)

Page 23
Aufgabe 2

Es ist kalt in Paris. Es schneit in New York. Es regnet in Venedig. Es ist heiß in Pisa. Es ist windig in London.

Page 24
Aufgabe 1

Name	isst gern	trinkt gern	Lieblingsfarbe	trägt
Anna	Tomaten	Cola	rot	pullover
Katrin	Bananen	Apfelsaft	gelb	Jeans
Dieter	Schinken	Mineralwasser	schwarz	T-Shirt
Hans	Eier	Milch	braun	Hose

Page 27
Aufgabe 1

(1)das Zebra (2) der Elefant (3) die Giraffe (4) das Nashorn (5) das Krokodil (6) das Känguruh (7) der Löwe

Page 34
Aufgabe 3

Herr Braun is 32 years old
Grandfather is 60 years old
Sarah is 10 years old
Jan is 8 years old
Nicklas is 6 years old
Frau Braun (Jan's mother) is 30 years old
Grandmother is 58 years old

Page 35
Aufgabe 1

His birthday is on Tuesday. He is 11 years old. His friends Marcus and Holger are coming to visit. If the weather is nice, they will have a picnic in the garden, with cola, lemonade, sandwiches, chocolate and lots of sweets. Everything he likes to eat and drink! Then they will play football.
If it rains they will have the picnic in the house and play with the computer.

Page 36
Aufgabe 1

Schokolade (Chocolate)
12 Eier (12 eggs)
6 Äpfel (6 apples)
ein Paket Zucker (1 packet of sugar)
1 Liter Cola (1 litre of cola)
2 Liter Limonade (2 litres of Lemonade)

Page 37
Aufgabe 1

Tomatensuppe
Pizza mit Tomaten und Gurken
Belegte Brote mit Leberwurst
Käse und Salat
Geburtstagskuchen

Aufgabe 2

Zucker (sugar), Eier (eggs), Mehl (flour), Kerzen (candles), Butter (butter), Schokolade (chocolate).

Page 38
Internet Challenge:

zwei, sieben, hunderteins, sieben, dreitausend, zwei, vier ein, acht, zehntausend.